NEW VANGUARD 323

TANKS AT THE IRON CURTAIN 1975–90

The ultimate generation of Cold War heavy armor

STEVEN J. ZALOGA   ILLUSTRATED BY FELIPE RODRÍGUEZ

OSPREY PUBLISHING

Bloomsbury Publishing Plc

Kemp House, Chawley Park, Cumnor Hill, Oxford OX2 9PH, UK

29 Earlsfort Terrace, Dublin 2, Ireland

1385 Broadway, 5th Floor, New York, NY 10018, USA

E-mail: info@ospreypublishing.com

www.ospreypublishing.com

OSPREY is a trademark of Osprey Publishing Ltd

First published in Great Britain in 2023

A catalog record for this book is available from the British Library.

ISBN: PB 9781472853806; eBook: 9781472853820;
ePDF 9781472853837; XML: 9781472853813

23 24 25 26 27 28   10 9 8 7 6 5 4 3 2 1

Index by Fionbar Lyons
Typeset by PDQ Digital Media Solutions, Bungay, UK
Printed and bound in India by Replika Press Private Ltd.

GLOSSARY

APFSDS	Armor-Piercing, Fin-Stabilized, Discarding-Sabot
ATGM	Antitank Guided Missile
ERA	Explosive Reactive Armor
FMBT	Future Main Battle Tank
GoF	Groups of Forces
GSFG	Group of Soviet Forces – Germany (*Gruppa sovetskikh voysk v Germanii*)
GSVG	(*see* GSFG)
HEAT	High-Explosive Antitank
IOC	Initial Operational Capability
LKZ	Leningrad Kirov Plant
MBT	Main Battle Tank
NATO	North Atlantic Treaty Organization
NERA	Non-Energetic Reactive Armor
NxRA	Non-explosive Reactive Armor
NII Stali	*Nauchno-issledovatelskiy institute Stali* (Scientific Research Institute for Steel)
RHA	Rolled Homogenous Armor
Ton	short ton (2,000lb)
Tonne	metric ton (1,000kg; 2,200lb)
USAREUR	US Army – Europe

AUTHOR'S NOTE

Unless otherwise noted, the photos here are from the author's collection.

CONTENTS

TANKS AT THE IRON CURTAIN 1975–90

The ultimate generation of Cold War heavy armor

INTRODUCTION

This book is the last of three to survey the tanks facing each other along the Iron Curtain from the end of World War II to the end of the Cold War. The first volume dealt with the tanks that remained in service from World War II, as well as the first generation of post-war tank designs. The second volume covered the next generation of tanks in 1960–75. This third volume covers the 1975–90 generations. Due to the large number of armies belonging to NATO and the Warsaw Pact, the focus is on the more consequential armies including the main protagonists and the forward deployed allies. In the case of the Warsaw Pact, greater attention is paid to the "Northern Tier" of East Germany, Poland, and Czechoslovakia, and less to the "Southern Tier" of Hungary, Romania, and Bulgaria. Likewise, coverage is greater for the major NATO armies such as the US Army, British Army, and Bundeswehr, and less on the smaller armies that did not manufacture their own tanks.

A few themes dominated tank development in the period of 1976–91. The 1973 war in the Middle East suggested that antitank guided missiles

The end of the Cold War led to some curious juxtapositions of former adversaries. Here, a Polish PT-91 Twardy tank takes part in NATO Exercise Saber Strike 17 at Adazi Training Grounds, Latvia alongside a US Marine M1A1 Abrams tank on June 9, 2017. The PT-91 was an upgraded version of the T-72M1 with explosive reactive armor. (US Marine Corps photo, 1st Lt Kristine Racicot)

(ATGM) would play a more important role on the future battlefield. This had significant technical effects in terms of the development of alternate forms of protection, such as explosive reactive armor (ERA) and non-energetic reactive armor (NERA). In addition, tank guns began to shift from the use of high-explosive antitank (HEAT) projectiles as their preferred anti-armor weapon to the new generation of armor-piercing, fin-stabilized, discarding-sabot (APFSDS) projectiles. More elaborate and expensive fire-control systems began to appear, including image-intensification and thermal imaging gunner sights, ballistic computers, and multi-axis gun stabilization.

THE TANKS, DOCTRINE, AND ORGANIZATION

Soviet Union

Soviet tank development took a conservative approach during the final years of the Cold War. The advent of the T-64 in the early 1970s set the pattern for later developments. Although there were numerous attempts to develop a revolutionary new tank, the Soviet Army remained focused on the evolutionary development of the T-64. The T-72 was an attempt to turn the basic T-64 design into a more robust and less expensive standard tank that would be economical enough for use by second-tier Soviet units, Warsaw Pact allies, and export customers. The third of the Soviet Triplet tanks was the T-80. Developed by the tank bureaucracy in Leningrad, the aim of this program was to switch the T-64 from diesel to gas-turbine propulsion. Like the early T-64, this program proved to be technically troublesome and controversial. As a result of the T-80's high costs and mechanical defects, the less radical T-72 became the dominant type during this period. To confuse matters further, when the Kremlin attempted to shift production at the Kharkov plant from the T-64 to the T-80, the Kharkov engineers managed to pressure the army to dump its controversial turbine engine in favor of a diesel engine, as used on the T-64B tank.

As a result of the bureaucratic shenanigans between the Kremlin, the regional governments, and the tank industry, by 1990 the Soviet Army was saddled with the Triplet tanks. Each shared very similar armor protection and firepower, but were beset with different logistical chains due to different powerplants, suspensions, and autoloaders. Critics later dubbed this situation to have been "a crime against the Soviet Army."

To simplify the logistics of deploying the Triplet tanks, the Soviet Army tried to concentrate specific types in the "Groups of Forces" (GoF) deployed in the central European satellite states. The T-80 gradually replaced the T-62 and T-64 in the Western Group of Forces (formerly Group of Soviet Forces – Germany until 1988) and the Northern Group of Forces in Poland. In 1990, the T-64 still equipped four of the divisions in Germany while the T-80 equipped 13 divisions. The T-64 remained in service in Hungary and the T-72 in Czechoslovakia. The picture in the western Soviet Union was considerably more complex since these regions had large numbers of tank training schools equipped with old

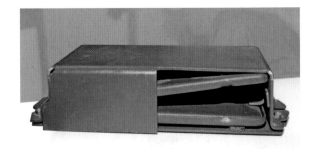

The Kontakt-1 reactive armor box contained two 4S20 explosive panels as shown in this cut-away.

types such as the T-55 and T-62. The Kiev Military District had a heavy concentration of T-64 tanks since this tank was manufactured within the district in Kharkov. The Belorussian Military District had a preponderance of T-72 tanks.

Forward-deployed Soviet tanks, 1990								
GoF, Military District*	Location	T-54	T-55	T-62	T-64	T-72	T-80	Total
Western GoF	Germany				1,096		2,967	4,063
Central GoF	Czechoslovakia					153		153
Northern Gof	Poland						598	598
Southern GoF	Hungary				214			214
Baltic MD	Baltic Rep.	14		309		66		389
Belorussian MD	Belarus	22		631	3	1,607		2,263
Carpathian MD	W. Ukraine	399	1,657	3	334	830		3,223
Kiev MD	Ukraine	210	186	188	1,804	56	141	2,585
Total		645	1,843	1,131	3,451	2,712	3,706	13,488

*GoF: Group of Forces; MD: Military District

One reason that the Soviet Army continued to favor the evolutionary approach in tank production was due to the high cost of mechanizing other elements of the Soviet Army. Besides acquiring new tanks, the Soviet Army was mechanizing its infantry regiments with the new BTR-70 armored personnel carrier, and the BMP-2 and BMP-3 infantry fighting vehicles. Its artillery regiments were shifting from towed to self-propelled artillery, and its air-defense units were adopting expensive new self-propelled missile systems. The airborne forces were also mechanizing their regiments with the BMD-2 air-droppable infantry fighting vehicle. Due to the sheer size of the Soviet Army, Moscow was forced to adopt economy measures during its force modernization programs of the 1980s. The arrival of Mikhail Gorbachev in 1985 led to the first serious effort to reconsider the amount of spending devoted to the Soviet Army. Gorbachev's reform efforts led to the reduction in tank production in the late 1980s. It also precipitated the eventual political collapse of the Warsaw Pact and the Soviet Union in 1989–91.

Countering the antitank missile

As was the case with NATO, the Soviet Army was well aware of the growing threat of antitank missiles even before the 1973 Middle-East War conclusively demonstrated their role on the modern battlefield. The shaped-charge warhead of these missiles could penetrate the homogenous steel armor used on most contemporary tanks. Besides the use of shaped-charge warheads on missiles, this was the technology used for NATO's most common type of antitank projectile, HEAT (high-explosive, antitank). The primary Soviet development agency for tank defense, NII Stali, had been working on various solutions to this problem including explosive-reactive armor (ERA), combination armor, and active protection systems (APS).

The T-55AD Drozd was the world's first service tank with an active defense system. The system included electronic sensors to identify incoming threats, and there were tubes for four 3UOF14 munitions on either side of the turret. Due to their cost, these were built in small numbers and only used by the Soviet Naval Infantry.

Although Soviet designers had considered the use of ERA since the late 1940s, the effort was revitalized in the early 1980s by NII Stali under the term "dynamic protection" (DZ: *dynamicheskaya zashchita*). NII Stali developed Kontakt-1 ERA consisting of two 4S20 panels mounted in a steel box. Each 4S20 panel consisted of a layer of explosive that propelled a steel plate into the path of the shaped-charge jet when detonated by an incoming warhead. There had been two main complaints about ERA. Some officers argued that it was only effective against shaped-charge warheads at a time when NATO was shifting to the use of APFSDS for tank-vs-tank fighting. Others argued that the added weight and cost did not justify its added protective values. The Israeli use of Blazer ERA in the 1982 Lebanon War overcame previous resistance to the adoption of this type of appliqué protection. Following testing in 1984–85, it was accepted for service use in 1985. NII Stali claimed it was about 15 percent more effective than Israeli Blazer ERA. Tanks with Kontakt-1 were given the suffix "V" to their designation, indicating *vzryvnoy* ("explosive").

In addition, NII Stali accelerated research on a second-generation "universal" ERA called Kontakt-5 which was intended to have some capability to degrade APFSDS projectiles as well as shaped-charge warheads. Kontakt-5 relied on a much more substantial steel plate on the outside of the 4S22 panel and this material was sufficient both to increase the degradation of shaped-charge jets, and also degrade APFSDS penetration by about 20–35 percent. This plate required a more energetic explosive insert with a TNT equivalent of 0.28kg in the 4S20 panels of Kontakt-1 versus 0.33kg in the 4S22 panels of the Kontakt-5. The Kontakt-5 panels had to be properly angled for maximum effect and in combination with their size and weight, they could not simply be bolted on as had been the case with Kontakt-1. Kontakt-5 had to be incorporated as a comprehensively designed armor package that would have to be undertaken during original manufacture or during capital rebuilding. As a result, Kontakt-1 and Kontakt-5 were distinguished from one another as appliqué ERA (*navesnoy DZ*) versus integrated ERA (*vstroenniy DZ*).

Combination armor had been developed in the late 1950s, and underwent continual improvement through 1990. During the late 1950s, a variety of laminate armors were studied to protect a tank's glacis plate. These usually consisted of a basic outer and inner layer of rolled homogenous steel armor with a sandwich of materials in between. Testing found that when a shaped-charge warhead detonated against a combination armor array, the hypersonic jet of metal particles was gradually bent and diverted as it passed through the laminate. The first of these, the T-64 glacis plate, consisted of a laminate of 80mm of steel armor on the outside followed by two 52mm layers of glass-reinforced plastic (*steklotekstol*) and a final 20mm layer of steel.

The T-55AM2 (Obiekt 157) upgrade package included the BDD "Brow" appliqué armor, and a laser rangefinder. Those further upgraded with the 1K13 guidance system for the Bastion guided projectile were designated T-55AM2B. The Czechoslovak T-55AM2 conversions, such as this one, used the Kladivo laser rangefinder instead of the Soviet KTD-2.

Turret protection was more complex since the front was round and could not rely on a simple flat plate. The cast turret of the T-64 had a cavity in the front and the combination armor began with an outer layer of 50mm of steel followed by 330mm of aluminum, and finally the inner layer of 100mm of cast steel. An improved alternative used on the T-64A suspended a matrix of ultra-porcelain balls (*Ultrafarfor*) in the cavity. Steel or aluminum was then poured into the cavity, enveloping the ceramic ball matrix. During test firing, the ceramic combination armor provided complete protection against 85mm and 100mm HEAT projectiles, 115mm APFSDS projectiles, as well as 75 percent protection from 115mm HEAT projectiles. This offered protection equivalent to about 550mm of steel in the turret front.

It was later discovered that in some cases the molten aluminum melted the wire and spring of the matrix, causing the balls to congregate at the bottom of the mold instead of being spaced evenly in the front. There was no practical way to determine when this had happened, so the ceramic ball composite armor was dropped in favor of other types of fillings. On the T-72A, the cavity was filled with sintered quartz. On the T-80B, the turret cavity was filled with ultra-porcelain rods in a matrix.

To protect the suspension, lightweight flipper panels, nicknamed *Eloshka* ("Christmas tree"), were developed using sheets of resin-impregnated fabric reinforced with thin steel plates. These folded against the tank during travel and then were flipped out in combat to shield the hull sides from frontal attack by shaped-charge warheads. They were first fitted to the T-64A in 1966 and were later used on the T-72 and T-80. The flipper plates were easily damaged and so, in 1980, they began to be replaced by full-length side skirts made of steel-reinforced rubberized fabric.

The combination turret armor eventually gave way to semi-active armor (*poluaktivnaya bronya*) intended to offer better protection against both HEAT and APFSDS. The turrets of the T-64B and the T-80U used a semi-active filled-cell armor (*bronya s yachestim napolnitelem*) developed by the Siberian branch of the Soviet Academy of Sciences. The cavity at the front of the turret consisted of two rows of polymer-filled cells backed by a steel plate and another layer of resin. When the cells were penetrated, shock waves reverberated in the semi-liquid filler in the cells, degrading the penetrator. This configuration was sometimes called non-explosive reactive armor (NxRA) in NATO.

The improved T-72 turret that entered production in 1983 used a different form of semi-active armor, more similar to the Chobham/Burlington non-energetic reactive armor (NERA) adopted by NATO. The new cast turret had an outer shell about 120mm thick of cast steel armor followed by a 400mm deep cavity backed by a final wall of 80mm cast steel armor. The cavity contained 20 special armor modules, each 30mm thick consisting of a 21mm steel plate, a 6mm thick rubber sheet, and a 3mm steel plate, followed by a 45mm steel plate. At its thickest point, the frontal armor was about 750mm thick. When struck,

The T-55A was upgraded with Kontakt-1 explosive reactive armor as the T-55AMV, as seen here. Those which were fitted with the V-46 engine upgrade were designated as the T-55AMV-1. This tank is fitted with the 1K13 guidance system in front of the gunner's hatch that was used with the Bastion guided projectile.

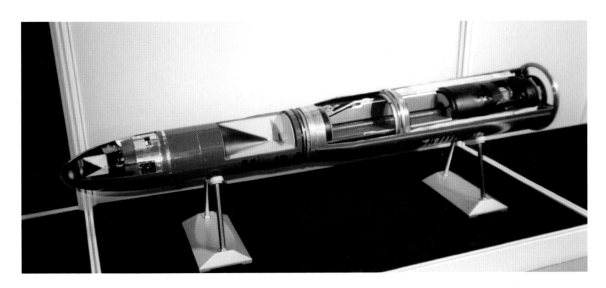

the rubber in the modules would compress, and then rebound, moving the steel plate back into the path of an incoming penetrator, degrading its potential penetration. The new turret offered the equivalent of 500–520mm of rolled homogenous armor against APFSDS and 600–620mm against HEAT warheads.

Modernizing the T-55

The T-55 was still in widespread Soviet service in the mid-1970s, and formed the backbone of the Warsaw Pact armies. There was growing interest to modernize these tanks, along with the similar T-62. This program accelerated after the Soviet invasion of Afghanistan in 1979. The tank units committed to Afghanistan were equipped mainly with the T-55 and T-62 which proved very vulnerable to RPG-7 antitank rockets and antitank mines. During the 1980 fighting, 16 percent of the tank losses were due to RPGs, and 59 percent to mines. On July 25, 1981, Moscow approved the modernization program as part of the 1981–85 five-year plan, authorizing the modification of 2,200 T-55 and 785 T-62 tanks through 1985. The Omsk tank plant managed the program, and the upgrade package was accepted for Soviet Army use in April 1983. The upgraded T-55 and T-55A tanks were designated respectively as the T-55M and T-55AM. This upgrade included passive appliqué armor, the Volna fire control upgrade, optional fitting of the new Bastion guided projectile, automotive upgrades, and numerous small improvements.

The appliqué armor was developed by NII Stali and was popularly known as "brow" armor (*brovi*) because the turret panels look like a pair of eyebrows when fitted to the tank. The glacis appliqué was an armored box filled with combination armor consisting of six layers of 5mm steel plate spaced 30mm apart with the cavity between filled with penapolyurethane resin. The

Guided tank projectiles fell out of favor in NATO in the 1980s, but remained popular in the Soviet Army. The 9K117-1 Bastion and the improved 9K117M1 Arkan (NATO: AT-10 Stabber) were adapted to a variety of guns in the 100–115mm range. The 9M117M1 missile seen here had a tandem shaped charge to strip away explosive reactive armor.

Estranged from the Warsaw Pact, Romania manufactured its own tanks derived from the T-55. This is a platoon of TR-85M1 Bizonul tanks from the 284th Tank Battalion, 282nd Mechanized Brigade, at the Smardan Training Area, Romania, during Exercise Danube Fury in December 2017. (US Army by Pfc Shelton Smith)

turret panels were cast armor, 60mm on the outer side, with a similar layered interior. The new turret armor increased the tank's protection from its basic 210mm thick steel to an equivalent of 380mm against kinetic energy projectiles and 450mm against shaped-charge projectiles. Side skirts were added to provide additional protection to the suspension and hull sides against shaped-charge warheads.

The T-64B Sosna had a variety of upgrades to the turret including the Kobra guidance antenna in front of the commander's cupola, the deletion of the right-side optics previously used by the TPD-2 optical rangefinder, and the enlarged 1G42 gunner's sight on the left side of the turret roof. The 2A46-2 gun was fitted with a thermal shroud around the barrel to reduce barrel warpage.

The Polish and Czechoslovak factories began a T-55 upgrade program paralleling the Soviet T-55M/T-55AM upgrade in 1984–89. These substituted locally developed fire control upgrade, the Czechoslovak package using the Kladivo system and the Polish upgrades using the Merida. The Warsaw Pact configurations were designated as T-55AM2 without the Bastion missile and T-55AM2B with the Bastion system. These upgrades were also applied to other Warsaw Pact T-55 tanks, notably the East German ones.

The king dethroned: the T-64B

By the mid-1970s, the T-64A was the premium tank of the Soviet Army. It equipped the forward deployed divisions in the Group of Soviet Forces – Germany (GSFG) alongside dwindling numbers of T-62 tanks. Numerous small improvements were made to the T-64A during its manufacture in the late 1970s, including the addition of a thermal jacket to the gun tube in August 1975.

The next major evolution of this tank was the T-64B. This program focused on the addition of a radio-command guided Kobra missile to provide long-range accuracy. A prototype fitted with the Kobra system was delivered in September 1969 but the program was delayed due to numerous technological problems associated with firing a complex guided missile out of a gun barrel at high speed. On August 12, 1973, the government approved the start of the Obiekt 447 Sosna ("pine tree") program to incorporate the Kobra system into an improved T-64A along with the 1A33 Ob fire control system. The T-64B Sosna was accepted for service on September 3, 1976. The

A

T-64A, WESTERN GROUP OF FORCES, SOVIET ARMY, GERMANY, 1989

In 1988, the Group of Soviet Forces – Germany was renamed as the Western Group of Forces (*Zapadnaya gruppa voisk*). Soviet units in Germany occasionally used tactical insignia but in the GSFG/WGF, they were not widely used on a day-to-day basis. They were most commonly applied during summer wargames, primarily for traffic control purposes. These were only temporary markings and were not permanently assigned to units. The most common Soviet tank marking was a three-digit side number (*Bortovoy nomer*). The Soviet numbering practice was deliberately non-standard and varied from division to division. The two most common patterns were to use the numbers in the sequence Battalion + Company + Tank, or Company + tank number (two digits). These tanks are in the usual camouflage green (*zashchitniy zeleno*), an extremely dark green when new; a US match is FS 34098.

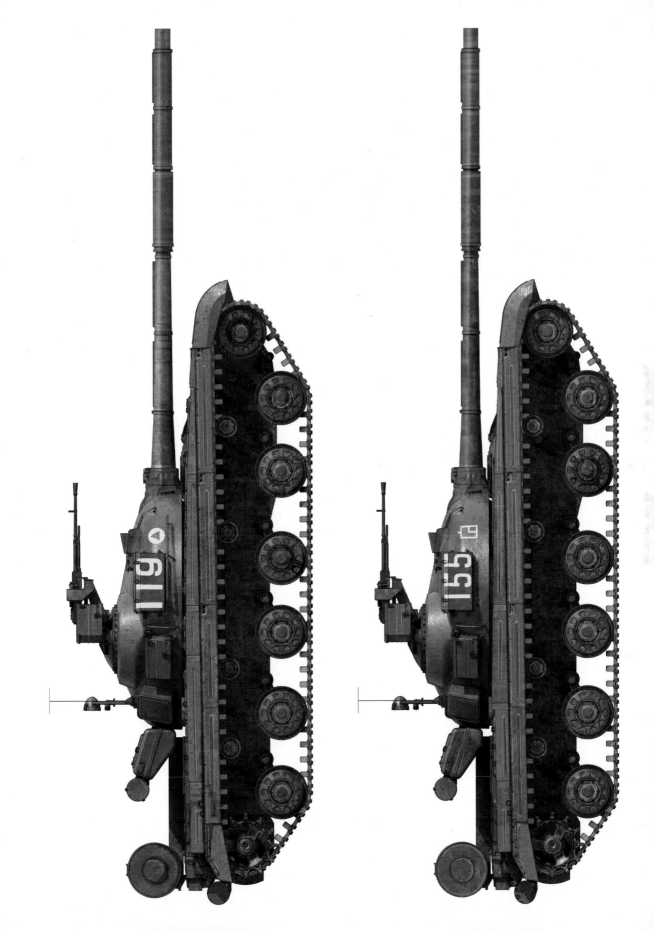

The T-64BV added 179 Kontakt-1 explosive reactive armor bricks. This upgrade effort started in 1985, though tanks in Germany often left off the bricks on the side skirts to facilitate suspension maintenance in peacetime.

advanced electronics in the T-64B led to a sharp price increase, from 194,000 rubles for the T-64A to 318,000 rubles for the T-64B gun-missile tank. Due to the high cost of the Kobra missile, the Sosna was manufactured in two configurations: the T-64B with the Kobra missile system, and the T-64B1 without the Kobra system.

NATO spotted the first forward-deployed T-64B with the Soviet Southern Group of Forces in Hungary in 1980 and in the Group of Soviet Forces – Germany in July 1981. When first deployed in Soviet tank regiments, the usual practice was to assign the T-64B to special "sniper" companies. Within each tank battalion, two companies would remain equipped with the T-64A, while a third company would receive the new T-64B "sniper tank." As in the case of the T-64A, there was continual upgrading of the T-64B during production. As was the case with other Soviet tanks, the T-64A and T-64B tanks were fitted with Kontakt-1 ERA and designated as T-64AV and T-64BV. The T-64BV began appearing in Germany in 1986, often replacing T-64A tanks in the 2nd Guards Tank Army and 3rd Shock Army. Manufacture of the T-64 tank ended in 1987.

The new premium tank: the T-80

Development of a turbine-powered version of the T-64 began in the early 1970s. As in the United States, the motivation behind the program was the promise of an exceptionally powerful engine with smaller volume than a conventional diesel tank engine. The Obiekt 219 entered troop trials in 1973 but engine durability was poor and fuel consumption was about 1.6 to 1.8 times higher than the diesel-powered T-64A.

The minister of defense, Marshal Andrei Grechko, was adamantly opposed to the Obiekt 219, arguing that it offered nothing over the existing T-64A other than higher speed, and this at a significantly higher cost both in terms of initial price and operating expense. The Obiekt 219 cost 480,000 rubles versus 143,000 rubles for the T-64A at the time. The Obiekt 219 might have been retired as another failed experiment but for Grechko's death in April 1976 and the appointment of Dmitry Ustinov in his place. He

had been one of the most ardent advocates of the conversion to gas-turbine propulsion since the mid-1960s, both for helicopters and tanks. As a result, on August 6, 1976, the Obiekt 219 was suddenly accepted for production under the army designation of T-80. Future tank production was scheduled to be shifted from the T-64 and T-72 to the T-80, and advanced tank designs such as Kharkov's T-74 were shelved.

The original production version of the T-80 (Obiekt 219 sp2) used a TPD-2-49 optical rangefinder.

The baseline T-80 was inferior to the T-64B in terms of fire controls and lacked the capability to fire guided tank projectiles. To redeem the design, the upgraded Obiekt 219R had the capability to fire the Kobra missile. At the same time, a new generation "Combination K" special armor was adopted for a new turret design that incorporated ultra-porcelain rods in the front turret cavity. The Obiekt 219R was accepted for Soviet service in 1978 as the T-80B and entered production at the Leningrad Kirov Plant (LKZ) after only a few hundred baseline T-80 tanks had been built. Production followed at the Omsk plant in 1979, replacing the T-55A that had remained in production there for export.

The T-80B became the most common production version of the T-80, and the first version to be forward deployed with the Group of Soviet Forces – Germany (GSFG) starting in 1981. The T-80B was first seen by NATO moving into Germany in April 1983 near Halle, beginning with the 29th Tank Regiment, 9th Tank Division of the 1st Guards Tank Army, and with units of the 8th Guards Tank Army in 1984. By 1985, each division in the 1st Guards Tank Army and 8th Guards Army had received some T-80B tanks. As described in detail below, the Soviet Army adopted explosive reactive armor in 1983. In 1985, the LKZ began to manufacture the T-80B with Kontakt as T-80BV, and some older tanks were retrofitted during periodic overhauls. The new reactive armor made the tanks largely invulnerable to frontal attack by standard NATO antitank missiles such as Dragon, Milan, TOW, and HOT. The T-80BV was deployed in Germany starting in 1986. At the time of the Soviet collapse in 1991, the T-80BV was the premium tank of the Soviet Ground Forces, deployed with the most combat-ready Soviet units in Germany and Poland.

The T-80B was the first version of the T-80 built in significant numbers. The T-80B can be externally distinguished from the earlier T-80 by the rectangular GTN-12 antenna for the Kobra missile system in front of the commander's cupola, as seen on this example preserved at the Central Artillery and Engineer Museum in St Petersburg.

In the late 1970s, the Kharkov plant had developed the T-64B with significantly improved fire controls and a new generation of armor. Rather than waste time transferring the features to a new T-80 turret, Moscow decided to merge the new Kharkov turret with the T-80B hull as the Obiekt 219A Olkha, and then to shift Kharkov's production from the T-64B to the T-80. As mentioned previously, the new turret used a semi-active filled-cell armor.

Although the Obiekt 219A was ready for production around 1982, serial production was delayed in order to incorporate a new generation of guided tank-gun projectile, the 9K119 Refleks, into the Obiekt 219V. The new Obiekt 219AS merged the features of Obiekt 219A and Obiekt 219V along with the new Kontakt-5 protective package. A pre-production batch of Obiekt 291AS tanks were completed in late 1983 for trials. The Obiekt 219AS was accepted for Soviet Army service in 1985 as the T-80U (U = *usovershenstvovanniy*: "improved") and went into series production at Omsk in 1987. Russian sources claim that Kontakt-5 plus the new turret armor provided protection equivalent to 780mm against APFSDS and 1,320mm against HEAT in the turret front. Although the T-80U was undoubtedly the best Soviet tank of its day, it came at a high price. A VNII Transmash study concluded that the T-80U was about 10 percent more combat effective than the T-72B, but cost about three times as much: 824,000 rubles compared to only 280,000 rubles. The T-80U was not forward deployed to Germany due to its late development.

Ustinov ordered the Kharkov plant to shift from T-64B to the T-80U. The Kharkov plant recommended the production of the T-80U with a diesel engine to cut down its costs and improve its reliability. Ustinov's views about turbine propulsion were not universally shared within the Soviet Army and a defense ministry study in 1984 concluded that for the next five-year plan, the Soviet Army could purchase 2,500 tanks and 6,000 Kharkov 6TD diesel engines, or 1,500 tanks and 2,000 GTD-1250 turbine engines. Ustinov's death in December 1984, followed by that of Leningrad party-boss Romanov in July 1985, removed the two most prominent supporters of the Leningrad turbine tank and cleared the way for a return to diesel tanks.

B **T-80BV, 65TH SEPARATE TANK BATTALION, 6TH GUARDS SEPARATE MOTOR RIFLE BERLIN BRIGADE, WESTERN GROUP OF FORCES, BERLIN, 1994**

Although Soviet tanks in Germany tended to be plainly finished, tanks were occasionally camouflage painted. This pattern was based on the Soviet engineer "Manual of Engineering Equipment and Methods for the Camouflage of Ground Forces." The manual suggested three different color combinations for verdant, winter, and desert conditions. This shows the verdant scheme as applied to a T-80BV tank battalion prior to its withdrawal from Germany in 1994. The pattern consisted of patches of grey and brown over the usual camouflage green. This type of camouflage painting was usually done by specialized engineer teams using a truck-mobile POS (*Polevoy okrasochnoy stanitsa*: "Field Painting Station"). Following the collapse of the Soviet Union, some units began to adopt distinctly Russian markings such as the Russian flag painted on a sheet metal plate on the turret side. Tactical markings usually included a three-digit side number (*Bortovoy nomer*), but in this case on the side skirts rather than the usual turret location.

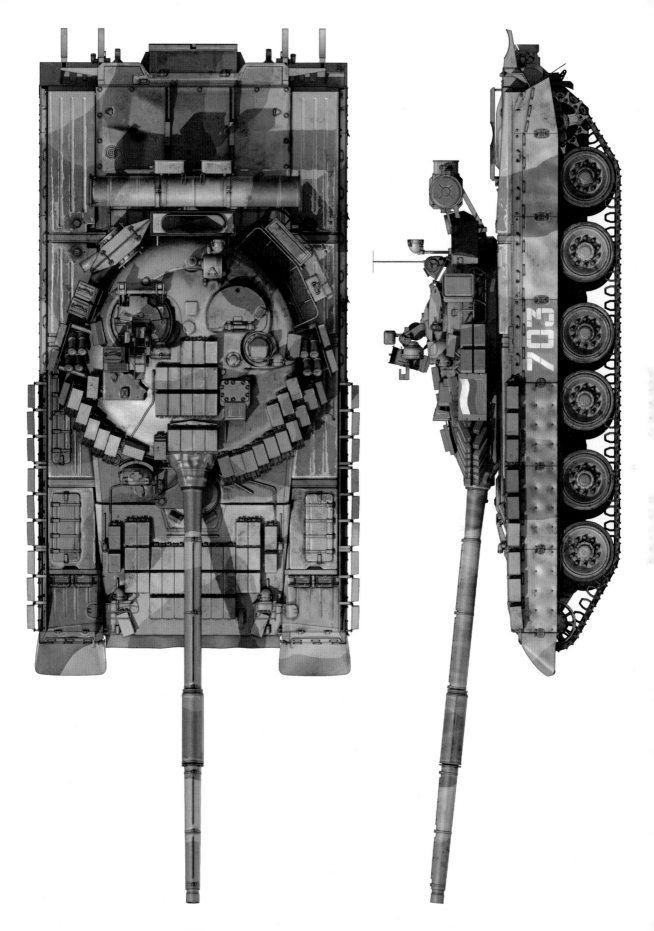

Government approval for the development of a diesel-powered T-80U was granted on September 2, 1985, and production was approved in 1986. There was some dispute over the designation of the new tank, with Kharkov recommending T-84 to follow the tradition of their T-34, T-44, T-54, and T-64 tanks. This proposal led to a bitter "fight under the carpet" between the industry and army with some detractors noting that the T-84 designation would draw attention to the fact that the Soviet Army was operating four different "standard" tanks – T-64, T-72, T-80, and T-84 – all with essentially the same characteristics except for four different power-plants. In the event, the less conspicuous designation T-80UD was selected, indicating "Improved Diesel" (*usovershenstvovanniy dieselniy*). The T-80UD was first deployed with the two "Kremlin court divisions," the 4th Guards Kantemirovskaya Tank Division and the 2nd Guards Tamanskaya Motor Rifle Division in the Moscow area. The T-80UD was first publicly shown at the May 9, 1990 Victory Day parade in Red Square in Moscow.

The T-80BV appeared in forward-deployed Soviet divisions in the second half of the 1980s, including two divisions in the Northern Group of Forces in Poland, the 6th Guards Vitebsk Motor Rifle Division in Pomerania and the 20th Zvenigorod Tank Division in Silesia. This example is seen on maneuvers in Poland. Notice that in peacetime the Kontakt-1 reactive armor bricks were not fitted to the side skirts.

Soviet tank production continued to decline in the late 1980s due to Gorbachev's attempts to rein in defense spending. The original 1989 plan had been for 3,739 T-80 and T-72 tanks but this was cut back, as was the 1990 plan.

Soviet production of the Triplet tanks				
	T-64	T-72	T-80	Total
1969–74	2,660	250		2,910
1975	700	700		1,400
1976	733	1,017	30	1,780
1977	875	1,150	40	2,065
1978	902	1,200	53	2,155
1979	910	1,360	80	2,350
1980	910	1,350	160	2,420
1981	910	1,445	278	2,633
1982	910	1,421	400	2,731
1983	880	1,520	540	2,940
1984	825	1,651	670	3,146
1985	633	1,759	770	3,162
1986	660	1,745	840	3,245
1987	600	1,794	860	3,254
1988		1,810	1,005	2,815
1989		1,148	710	1,858
1990		776	630	1,406
Total	**13,108**	**22,096**	**7,066**	**42,270**

T-72: the mobilization tank

Development of an improved T-72 began in May 1975. The original T-72 was inferior to the T-64A in protection. Although it shared the same glacis plate with combination armor, the turret was homogenous cast steel, lacking the aluminum or ceramic insert used in the T-64A turret. A number of different protection options were tested, finally settling on the 172.10.073SB Kvartz turret which added a sintered quartz filler (*peschanye sterzhni*) in front cavities of the turret. This

feature entered production during the final production run of the baseline T-72 tanks at Nizhni-Tagil in July 1978 and was nicknamed the "Dolly Parton" in NATO.

The T-80U was the final Cold War version of the Soviet Army's premium tank. This featured the new Kontakt-5 explosive reactive armor.

Although the design bureau at Nizhni-Tagil proposed a wide range of upgrades to the T-72, this was resisted by defense minister Dmitry Ustinov. He viewed the T-72 as a second-rate mobilization tank suitable for second-tier units and for export. He favored a conversion of the Nizhni-Tagil plant to the T-80. Proposals for expensive T-72 options, such as guided projectiles and advanced fire controls, were rejected in favor of the premium tanks such as the T-64A and T-80.

In conjunction with the turret armor improvements, the T-72 upgrade program examined modest fire control improvements. The TPD-2-49 optical rangefinder was replaced by the TPD-K1 laser rangefinder in the late production T-72 (172M sb4) in 1978. New production tanks with the full upgrade package were designated T-72A and entered production at Nizhni-Tagil in September 1978; it was formally accepted for service on June 22, 1979.

A series of incremental upgrades continued on the T-72A including steel-reinforced rubber side skirts in January 1979 on the T-72A (172M sb6). An improved combination armor for the glacis plate entered production in October 1979 that switched from the original 80mm steel–105mm GRP–20mm steel sandwich to a 60–105–50mm sandwich. Tests of Israeli M111 105mm APFSDS projectiles obtained by the Soviet Army in the wake of the 1982 Lebanon War suggested that the glacis plate was still vulnerable. As a short-term solution, a 16mm steel appliqué plate was added to the front of the glacis plate starting in 1983.

A program to modernize the T-72A began in July 1981 as Izdeliye 184. The turret armor was substantially revised by the use of semi-active armor as described earlier. The new turret offered the equivalent of 500–520mm of rolled homogenous armor against APFSDS and 600–620mm against HEAT warheads. Limited production of the new turrets began on July 1, 1983, alongside the earlier Kvartz turret on late-production T-72A tanks. The complete switch to the new turret took place on January 1, 1984. This version was nicknamed the "Super Dolly Parton" in NATO.

Unlike the T-64 and T-80, the initial production versions of the T-72 could not fire guided projectiles such as the Kobra missile. In March 1982,

The initial T-72 Ural-1 tank used a TPD-2-49 optical rangefinder evident from the sight mount in front of the commander's station on the right side of the turret roof. The early production series lacked a thermal sleeve over the gun tube as seen on this example.

The T-72A had a number of upgrades, most notably combined frontal turret armor. The substitution of a TPD-K1 laser rangefinder in place of the previous optical rangefinder is a visual cue to this variant. This series had many other smaller improvements including the Type 902 Tucha smoke launchers on the turret front.

work began on the Izdeliye 177 that was fitted with the new 9K120 Svir missile system and in February 1983 a study began on the Izdeliye 179 with the Kobra missile system. In February 1984, operational trials were conducted of the various upgrades to the T-72A.

A formal start of production of the T-72B was on November 27, 1984. The T-72B had the new 9K120 Svir missile system, the new 172.10.100SB turret adapted to mount the new 1K13-49 gunner's sight, Kontakt-1 ERA, the improved 2A46M 125mm gun, and the uprated 840hp V-84-1 engine. Some of the final production batches of T-72A manufactured in 1983–84 had some of the features associated with the T-72B including the new turret, but lacked the Svir missile system and the Kontakt-1. In December 1985, production of the T-72B1 began and was completed in September 1989. It was the same as the T-72B but lacked the Svir missile system to reduce the cost of the tank.

Armor protection on the T-72B continued with an improved configuration of semi-active armor in the casting of a new turret. The glacis armor was also changed, with the gap between the outer and inner steel armor plates now filled with four spaced steel plates of 10–10–20–20mm instead of the GRP sandwich used in earlier configurations. These armor upgrades were introduced into T-72B production in October 1987.

The final upgrade package for the T-72B was dubbed T-72B Usovershenstvovanniy ("Improved"; 188 SB; T-72BM). This substituted the new Kontakt-5 ERA for the Kontakt-1. Various other upgrades were tested including the improved 2A66 Anker 125mm gun, the Shtora anti-missile optical jammer, and the Agava thermal imaging gunner's sight. Production of the T-72B tank at Nizhni-Tagil formally ended on November 13, 1991. A small production run of the T-72BM (188-1) with Kontakt-5 took place prior to the collapse of the USSR, but many of the other upgrades did not occur until the advent of the re-named T-90 in August 1991.

The T-72 export tank

In 1976, the Kremlin selected the T-72 as the next export tank for Soviet clients, especially the Warsaw Pact allies. Both Poland and Czechoslovakia were still manufacturing the T-55A tank in the early 1980s even though it was clearly obsolete. The first T-72 export tank manufactured in Nizhni-Tagil was internally designated as Izdeliye 172M-E (E = *eksportniy*: "export") and these tanks were sold to Warsaw Pact armies as well as to India and customers in the Middle East starting in 1978. These were essentially similar to the original Soviet

T-72 with the optical rangefinder and homogenous steel turret armor.

License production agreements were reached with the Warsaw Pact countries in 1978. Production of the T-72 (172M-E) began at Poland's Bumar-Łabędy plant and at Czechoslovakia's Martin plant in 1982 in place of the T-55A.

A further export version, the T-72M (Obiekt 172M-E2) began development in 1978 and production for export clients began at Nizhni-Tagil around 1980, and in Poland and Czechoslovakia in 1985. The T-72M was a hybrid between the Soviet T-72 and T-72A in features. For example, it used the TPD-K1 laser rangefinder as found on the T-72A, but it was still fitted with the monolithic steel turret of the baseline T-72. The initial T-72M production version, the Izd. 172M-E2, had the original 2A46 125mm gun without the thermal shroud, and still carried the basic ammunition load of 39 rounds for the main gun. It was followed by the Izd. 172M-1-E3 which added a thermal sleeve to the 125mm gun, increased the ammunition stowage from 39 to 44 rounds, introduced the improved TNP-1-49-23 night sight, added the Tucha smoke grenade launchers to the front of the turret, and added the anti-HEAT side skirts. The final production model, the T-72M1 (172M1-E5), was approved in 1982. This was a close analog to the Soviet T-72A, with the upgraded turret with quartz filler and an upgraded glacis plate with a 16mm steel appliqué. Production of the T-72M1 began in Poland and Czechoslovakia in 1986.

Poland built 1,610 T-72 of all variants, of which over 600 were delivered to the Polish Army and the remainder exported. For example, a large fraction of Iraqi T-72 tanks came from Poland. Through 1991, Czechoslovakia manufactured 1,782 T-72 tanks, of which 864 went to the army and 918 were exported. The majority of T-72 tanks in the Warsaw Pact came from Polish and Czechoslovak exports. For example, of the 552 T-72 tanks in the East German Army, 135 came from the Soviet Union, 260 from Czechoslovakia, and 157 from Poland.

Romania was an outlier in the Warsaw Pact tank program. The invasion of Czechoslovakia by the Warsaw Pact in 1968 led to the final estrangement of Romania from the bloc, and a shift to local industry to supply the Romanian Army. In 1972, the government approved a program to build a medium tank, based roughly on the T-55. The new tank was designated TR-77 (Tanc românesc model 1977). The original plan was to build the tank around a German engine, but when Berlin refused the export license, a copy of the Soviet 580hp V-55 engine was chosen. As a result, the tank was

The T-72A Mod. 1983 retained the Kvartz turret but had other upgrades including additional anti-radiation panels on the turret roof and the Type 902 Tucha smoke dispensers. These tanks took part in the Zapad maneuvers in the western USSR.

The final production T-72A tanks built in 1983–84 were fitted with the new turret with semi-active armor. This can be easily confused with the early-production T-72B but lacked Kontakt-1 reactive armor and the Svir guided projectile system. This is an example with the 2nd Guards Tamanskaya Motor Rifle Division on parade in Moscow in 1988.

The T-72B (Izd. 188 sb-1) had the new turret with semi-active armor, Kontakt-1 reactive armor, and the Svir missile system including the new 1K13-49 gunner's sight. This particular tank is a prototype of the T-72S Shilden, the export variant of the T-72B that had two fewer rows of ERA bricks on the hull side.

also called the TR-580. Production began in 1979 and continued until 1985 by which time about 495 had been delivered to the Romanian Army. It was first deployed with the 9th Motor Rifle Division.

Romania ordered 30 T-72 tanks from the USSR in 1978 but a proposal to begin license production in Romania was rebuffed by Moscow. As a result, the TR-77-580 design was upgraded into the TR-85-800. This was powered by an 800hp diesel engine. A total of 591 TR-85s were built through 1990. Although strongly influenced by Soviet tank designs and using copies of some Soviet components, the Romanian tanks were largely an indigenous design with many different technical features.

Romania made an effort to reverse-engineer the T-72 and built several prototypes of the TR-125 tank starting in 1987. At the end of the Cold War, this project was canceled before any serial production was undertaken. Instead, the TR-85 tanks were modernized into the TR-85M1 Bizonul (bison) beginning in the mid-1990s.

C T-72M1, NATIONALE VOLKSARMEE, 1989

In the early 1960s, the East German National Volksarmee (NVA) switched its basic vehicle camouflage color from Feldgrau Nr. 3 to Olivgrün 2425. This paint was sometimes called Chlorbuna Grün due to the method of its manufacture by Kombinat Lacke und Farben (LACUFA). It tended to fade to a lighter and less saturated green than other Warsaw Pact camouflage green. In the late 1980s, the NVA began to switch to a three-color summer camouflage that was codified in April 1988 in manual K 052/3/016 *Verzerrungsanstriche an Kampftechnik, Bewaffnung und Ausrüstung.*" The summer disruptive scheme was based on Olivgrün 2425 covering roughly half of the surface, and spray-painted with patterns of Dämmergrau 2403 (dusky grey) and Schwarzgrau 2402 (black-grey), each covering roughly a quarter of the surface. These colors corresponded roughly to current German color standards RAL 6003 (green), RAL 7001 (silver grey), and RAL 9005 (black). The new color schemes began to be applied in 1988, but the NVA never released paint guidelines for the tank patterns, leaving the troops to their own discretion. Not all units had received sufficient paint and equipment to camouflage their tanks by the time the NVA was dissolved in 1990.

Soviet Army tanks by sub-type, Atlantic-to-the-Urals, 1990

T-54	1
T-54B	925
T-54M	667
T-54 sub-total	**1,593**
T-55	542
T-55A	957
T-55AD	258
T-55AMV	40
T-55M	1,006
T-55MV	145
T-55 sub-total	**2,948**
T-62	1,665
T-62M	243
T-62MV	113
T-62 sub-total	**2,021**
T-64R	578
T-64A	1,606
T-64B	1,632
T-64BV	166
T-64 sub-total	**3,982**
T-72	1,501
T-72A	959
T-72B	1,211
T-72B1	1,421
T-72 sub-total	**5,092**
T-80	112
T-80B	3,737
T-80BV	617
T-80U	410
T-80 sub-total	**4,876**
Total	**20,512**

Soviet tanks: Atlantic-to-the-Urals by deployment, 1990

	T-54	T-55	T-62	T-64	T-72	T-80	Total
Group of Forces, Mil. Districts	1,159	2,220	1,170	3,587	4,919	4,595	17,650
Training units	31	71	88	60	190	175	615
Repair plants	408	834	454	332	294	97	2,419
Naval Infantry	0	0	0	271	271	271	813
Total	**1,598**	**3,125**	**1,712**	**4,250**	**5,674**	**5,138**	**21,497**

Warsaw Pact tank inventory, 1990

	T-34-85	T-54	T-55	Other	T-72	Total
Bulgaria	670		1,141		334	2,145
Czechoslovakia		373	527		897	1,797
Germany (DDR)	22	198	1,589		551	2,360
Hungary	72	148	987		138	1,345
Poland			2,093		757	2,850
Romania	1,059		757	1,004*	30	2,850
Total	**1,823**	**719**	**7,094**	**1,004**	**2,707**	**13,347**

*591 TR-85 + 413 TR-580

United States
The M60 tank

The M60A1 was the principal US Army tank in 1975, with the production variant being the M60A1 RISE (Reliability Improved Selected Equipment). The US Army realized that the M60A1 was dated, but the failure of the MBT-70 replacement program and a shortage of development funds due to the Vietnam War delayed the production of a replacement.

The final production variant of the M60A1 series was the M60A1 RISE Passive that introduced new image-intensification night viewing equipment, the AN/VVS-2 for the driver and the M35E1 gunner's periscope. Image-intensification was a significant step forward in night fighting, since it was entirely passive and did not require illumination by infrared searchlights. The sights amplified ambient moonlight and starlight in order to provide an image. Production of the M60A1 RISE Passive continued until 1980 with the debut of the M60A3.

A Polish T-72M of the 11 Drezdeńska Dywizja Pancerna in the initial configuration with the "gill" armor panels over the suspension. In combat, these would be flipped outward to serve as stand-off protection from shaped-charge warheads.

The M60A3 represented a substantial improvement to the fire controls of the M60A1 tank. This tank was the world's first to be fitted with a thermal imaging gunner's sight, the AN/VSG-2 TTS (Tank Thermal Sight). As in the case of image-intensification night sights, the TTS was entirely passive, but sensed infrared wavelengths rather than light in the visible spectrum. This was advantageous for tank fighting since the image-intensification sights had mediocre performance on moonless nights or when cloud cover blocked starlight. The thermal sight worked under all weather and light conditions. Also, it facilitated target acquisition since an enemy tank gave off more infrared energy than the natural background, not only due to its engine, but also due to infrared heat energy from tracks, wheels, and residual daytime heating. As a result, enemy tanks tended to stand out from the background in a clearer fashion than when using image intensification sights. This new generation of tank electronics considerably increased tank prices, with the TTS accounting for more than a quarter of the price of the tank.

Bulgaria obtained the bulk of its T-72 tanks from other Warsaw Pact countries such as Czechoslovakia. This is a column of Bulgarian T-72M1 tanks during training exercise Eagle Sentinel 17, at Novo Selo Training Area, on July 12, 2017. (US DoD by PO 2nd Class Christopher Lange)

Besides the TTS, the M60A3 introduced fire control upgrades including the M21 solid-state computer, a muzzle reference system, a cross-wind sensor, and the AN/VVG-2 laser rangefinder. There were also a number of other improvements including tube-over-bar suspension upgrades, a halon fire extinguisher, reconfiguration of the ammunition to reduce its vulnerability, smoke grenade dischargers, and a thermal shroud for the gun barrel. By March of 1980, about 335 M60A3s had been completed but they had not

An M60A3 of the "Iron Dukes," 3-32 Armor, passes through the village of Langgöns in West Germany during the Reforger '85 exercise with the steeple of the Evangelische Jakobuskirche in the background. The Iron Dukes served with Force Orange during the maneuvers, hence the temporary exercise markings.

An M60A3 of 4-69 Armor in temporary winter camouflage during Central Guardian, a phase of Exercise Reforger '85, on January 22, 1985, near Giessen, West Germany. This unit took part in the exercise with Force Blue, and so had temporary blue maneuver markings.

been issued to units due to delays in the manufacture of the new fire control systems.

The US Army planned to upgrade all of its M60A1 tanks to M60A3 standards but, in 1984, this was reduced due to a decision to cap the M60A3 fleet at 5,400 tanks. This left about 1,950 M60A1 tanks in war-reserve. Although all US Army M60A3 tanks were fitted with the TTS thermal sight, some M60A1 tanks were upgraded to M60A3 standards for export, minus the TTS. These were designated as M60A3 Passive, referring to their image intensification sights, while tanks fitted with TTS sometimes were called M60A3 TTS. The last M60A3s for the US Army were produced in 1985, but M60A3 production continued until 1987 for export customers including Egypt and Saudi Arabia.

New generation: the M1 Abrams

The US had intended to replace the M60 tank with the MBT-70, a joint venture with Germany that began in 1963. This program was canceled in December 1969 due to the extremely high price of the tank, over $850,000. The US Army attempted to develop an austere variant, the XM803 at a unit cost of $600,000, but this was canceled by Congressional action in December 1971 due to concern that the tank was too sophisticated and too expensive. The MBT-70 program took place in the midst of the Vietnam War, and as a result, the US Army suffered from severe budget constraints for new equipment. In January 1972, the New Main Battle Tank (NMBT) program began.

An MBT Task Force under Maj Gen William Desobry concluded that a new tank was needed due to deficiencies in the M60A1 tank compared to contemporary Soviet tanks such as the T-62. The M60A1 suffered from an excessive silhouette, inadequate acceleration and cross-country speed, unacceptable reliability of the powertrain and armament system, lack of adequate firepower on the move, and insufficient ballistic protection against modern APFSDS projectiles.

The new tank was designated as the XM1 and the development program began in January 1973. The cost objective was put at $507,790 ($FY72) for a production run of 3,312 tanks. By way of comparison the M60A1 tank cost $339,000 at the time. Unlike previous US tanks since the 1950s, the XM1 was competitively designed by industry rather than by US Army agencies.

As in the case of the Soviet Union, there was considerable interest in examining the advantages of gas-turbine propulsion compared to traditional diesel engines. As a result, the Chrysler XM1 prototype was fitted with the AVCO-Lycoming AGT-1500 gas turbine while the General Motors prototype was fitted with the AVCR-1360 diesel.

Several armament options for the XM1 were examined including the existing M68 105mm gun, a British 110mm gun, and the German Rheinmetall 120mm gun. By 1975, the US Army concluded that the German 120mm gun was best-suited to meet the long-term threat. However, the baseline threat was considered to be the Soviet T-62 tank. The 105mm gun with new ammunition was considered adequate in the short term to deal with this threat, and the 105mm option kept the XM1 under its price objectives. In January 1976, the Pentagon approved the army decision to stick with the 105mm gun in the initial production series of the XM1.

The XM1 requirements called for armor protection against the Soviet T-62 tanks' 115mm APFSDS projectile at 800–1,200 meters and the AT-3 Sagger missile's 127mm HEAT warhead over a 50-degree frontal arc. Side protection was sufficient to defeat the RPG-7 rocket launcher at 45 degrees on the crew compartment sides and at all angles against the turret side. Both of the initial XM1 designs used conventional steel armor.

In the mid-1980s, the US Army completed the development of an explosive reactive armor kit for the M60 tank. Officially called Appliqué Armor, it consisted of 52 M1 and 43 M2 armor tiles. This is one of the prototypes of the kit fitted to an M60A3 tank. In the event, it was not widely deployed by the US Army since the M60A3 was being replaced by the M1 Abrams tank in regular army battalions.

Since 1964, the British Army's FVRDE (Fighting Vehicles Research and Development Establishment) facility at Chobham had kept the US Army informed about its research on Burlington "special armor." This was an evolving armor package consisting of non-energetic reactive armor (NERA) modules with spaced laminates of steel and other materials fitted over conventional welded steel armor. Burlington offered much superior performance to steel armor in the defeat of shaped-charge HEAT warheads, while at the same time being equivalent to conventional steel armor in defeating APFSDS kinetic energy penetrators. The UK and the US began discussions on a memorandum of understanding about the development and use of Burlington armor in 1969, but plans to incorporate it into the XM1 design did not begin until 1973 after the start of the program. A major incentive for adopting Burlington armor was the Israeli combat experience in the 1973 Yom Kippur War. The Israeli tank force suffered heavy losses at the hands of RPG-7 antitank rocket launchers and AT-3 Sagger (9M14M Malyutka) antitank missiles. The initial pilots of the XM1 program during the validation phase had conventional steel armor, but the turrets and hull were redesigned. These featured an improved version of Burlington armor developed in conjunction between the FVRDE and the Ballistics Research Lab (BRL) at Aberdeen Proving Ground (APG) in Maryland under the codename Green Grape.

Besides the armor package, the XM1 designs incorporated an ammunition bustle at the rear of the turret that separated most of the ammunition from the fighting compartment by sliding blast-doors. Should the ammunition be

The M1 Abrams main battle tank was first deployed in significant numbers in 1982. One of the first units equipped was the 2nd Armored Division at Fort Hood, Texas. These are from 3-67th Armor.

set afire, the blast doors would protect the crew long enough to escape, and in many cases would slow or prevent the spread of a catastrophic fire into the rest of the tank.

The developmental and operational trials of the pilot tanks were conducted at APG in January–May 1976. This was followed by trials of the German Leopard IIAV in the autumn of 1976. The Leopard II was judged to have superior fire controls, but inferior armor, ammunition compartmentalization, and gun traverse. It was estimated that the Leopard IIAV would cost about 25 percent more than either of the American competitors if built in the USA and so it was withdrawn from consideration.

The initial pilot designs were upgraded including provisions to allow the future use of the German 120mm gun and to employ the Green Grape NERA. The modified Chrysler design was selected on November 12, 1976 to proceed to full-scale engineering-manufacturing development. Subsequent trials of the upgraded Chrysler XM1 pilot tanks were satisfactory enough that a limited-rate-initial-production contract was awarded in May 1979 for the first 110 tanks. The first production tank was delivered in February 1980 and the tank was type classified as the M1 tank in February 1981. It was named after Creighton Abrams, the army chief-of-staff during the latter part of the Vietnam War, and a World War II tanker. By the summer of 1982, 585 tanks had been delivered, all trials had been completed, and five battalions of M1 tanks deployed, three in Europe and two in the US. The last basic M1 was completed in January 1985.

Alongside the development of the XM1 tank, there was a parallel effort to develop improved tank ammunition for its M68A1 gun. An APFSDS projectile using a depleted uranium penetrator, the 105mm M774, entered service in the summer of 1981 followed by the improved M833 in the autumn of 1983. There was also a new 105mm HEAT round, the M815, that entered service in the spring of 1987.

By the time the M1 tank entered serial production, it was evident that the decision to employ the 105mm gun was a mistake forced on the army by budget considerations. Evidence of the new T-64A tank began to emerge in the early 1970s, and, by 1976, two divisions in East Germany had been re-equipped with the type. Fortunately, provisions had been incorporated into the turret design to adopt the German 120mm gun. As a result, the M1E1 program began in June 1979. The German gun was adapted to American manufacturing techniques and the first example of the XM256 120mm gun delivered in April 1980.

An M1 Abrams of the 11th Cavalry taking part in the Reforger '83 maneuvers in Germany as part of Force Blue. This tank is fitted with the MILES laser training system including the gunfire simulator over the gun barrel and the laser detector strip around the turret. (US Army)

A variety of other improvements were developed as part of the M1E1 upgrade including a new version of Green Grape special armor to deal with the Soviet 125mm tank gun, a hybrid NBC (Nuclear, biological, chemical) protective system, a micro-cooling vest for operations in hot weather, and a variety of suspension, transmission, and final drive upgrades. Details of the upgraded special armor package remain secret, but a Soviet report assessed the armor protection of the M1A1 against APFSDS to be equivalent to 600mm RHA (rolled homogenous armor) compared to 470mm for the M1, and 700mm against HEAT compared to 650mm for the basic M1. The first M1E1 pilots were delivered in March 1981.

While awaiting the completion of M1E1 development, the army decided to begin switching over the production line to the M1E1 features, but without the new 120mm gun or NBC suite. The resulting version was the IPM1 (Improved Product M1) that entered production in October 1984. The first IPM1 tanks were deployed with 2-69 Armor at Fort Benning in early 1985.

The M1E1 was type classified as the 120mm Gun Tank M1A1 in December 1984 and the first production tanks were delivered in August 1985. By 1986, all production tanks for the US Army were in this configuration. Priority for the new tank went to the US Army Europe (USAREUR) which began receiving them in large numbers by 1988.

The Green Grape special armor continued to evolve, including the incorporation of depleted uranium in the sandwich. This is a metallic uranium consisting of isotopes that emit little or no radiation. The principal advantage of uranium is its weight and density, about double that of lead per volume. The variant incorporating the third-generation special armor was dubbed the M1A1 HA (HA = heavy armor). Besides being incorporated into new production tanks starting in October 1988, the heavy armor package could also be retrofitted to existing IPM1 and M1A1 tanks. The M1A1 and M1A1 HA were the principal types of Abrams used in the 1991 war with Iraq. Total US M1A1 production was 4,771 tanks. Development of the M1A2 tank began in 1989 and it was adopted for service in April 1994. Planned production of the M1A2 was substantially trimmed due to the end of the Cold War.

Priority for the new M1A1 Abrams went to the US Army Europe (USAREUR) which began receiving it in large numbers by 1988. It saw its combat debut in 1991 during Operation *Desert Storm*. This is an M1A1 tank fitted with a Track Width Mine Plow of the 24th Infantry Division (Mechanized) at Fort Stewart, Georgia, shortly after its return from the Gulf War in 1991.

The M8 Buford Armored Gun System

The US Army began the development of a new light tank to replace the M551 Sheridan in 1983, called the Armored Gun System (AGS). The program suffered considerable delay due to budget problems and confusion over the technical requirements. The original objective was for about 600 tanks for the 82nd Airborne Division, 2nd Armored Cavalry, and a number of other units. Formal requirements were finally issued in April 1990 based in part on the experiences of the M551 in Panama and Operation *Desert Storm*. The request to industry was released in 1991 and an FMC Corp. design was selected as the XM8 AGS from the various offerings in June 1992. After further development and testing, it was accepted for the army in October 1995 as the M8 Buford AGS. The program lasted only a few more months before being canceled in January 1996 due to budgetary reasons.

D

IPM1, D COMPANY, 4-8 CAVALRY, 3RD ARMORED DIVISION, CENTAG TEAM, CAT '87, BERGEN-HOHNE, FRG, 1987

The winning platoon at the 1987 Canadian Army Trophy was from the US Army's 4-8 Cavalry. It adopted the discombobulated "Bill the Cat" from cartoonist Berkeley Breathed's popular "Bloom County" comic strip as its mascot. This was an inside poke at one of its US rivals, 3-64 Armor, who had been using the comic-strip cat Garfield as its mascot. The team also applied a version of its competition patch on the right front side of the turret along with a 3rd Armored Division "Spearhead" emblem on a metal plate on the turret basket. A US flag decal was carried on the side skirts, and a Canadian flag on the turret bin. The Canadian flag was in recognition of the close training between the team and the Royal Canadian Dragoons. Aside from the CAT '87 markings, US Army tactical markings during this period were very austere. Bumper codes at front and rear were supposed to be painted black. Since this wasn't visible on the base color of Forest Green, the bumper codes were painted on sand-colored rectangles. The tank name "DANGER ZONE" was painted on the fume extractor, a reference to the Kenny Loggins song from the popular *Top Gun* movie. Platoons were sometimes identified by the white bands on the front of the gun barrel. Temporary identification boards were often attached to the turret bustle rack, in this case, a large letter A.

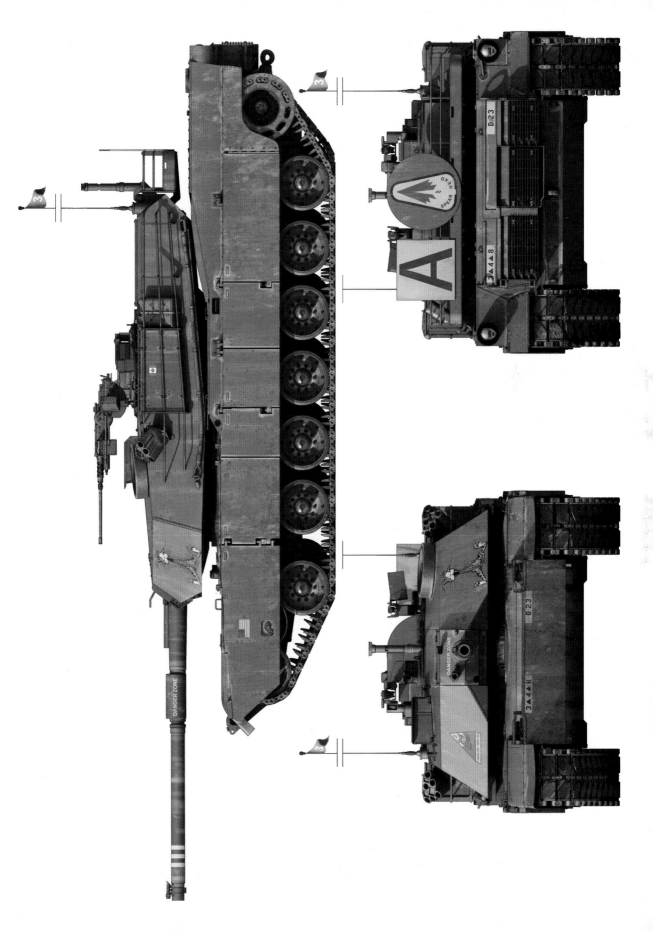

US tank production, 1975–90					
	M60A1	M60A3	M1	M1A1	Total
1975	682				682
1976	885				885
1977	981				981
1978	1,179	19			1,198
1979	668	450			1,118
1980	21	786	16		823
1981		523	157		680
1982		349	439		788
1983		382	754		1,136
1984		268	777		1,045
1985		298	594	280	1,172
1986				529	529
1987		94		996	1,090
1988				819	819
1989				725	725
1990				718	718
Total	**4,416**	**3,169**	**2,737**	**4,067**	**14,389**

Germany
Leopard 2

The collapse of the MBT-70 program prompted Germany to begin studies for a future tank. The initial prototypes of the Leopard 2 were delivered in 1973 with a 105mm gun. Over 20 prototypes were built to permit the examination of a variety of hull, turret, and sub-component configurations. Prototype PT 07 was sold to the US Army and testing started in 1973. Germany hoped to enter into a partnership with other NATO countries and besides the joint efforts with the USA, there were also discussions over a Future Main Battle Tank (FMBT) with Britain.

The lessons of the 1973 Middle-East War led to some concern that the turret armor was not adequate, a viewpoint that was reinforced by the US Army testing the Leopard 2 prototype. Germany was aware of the British research at Chobham into Burlington armour from the FMBT discussions. The switch from conventional armor to Burlington NERA required the design to breach the initial weight limits, going from 50 to 60 tonnes.

In 1974, Germany discussed a potential joint program with the US, offering the Leopard 2AV (austere version). In spite of the eventual rejection of the Leopard 2 for the US Army due to its higher cost, a company study of the program later noted that the US tests "provided valuable information from which the German side benefited considerably." Besides the technical interchange with the US Army, Germany also

Development of the Armored Gun System light tank began in the early 1980s as a replacement for the M551 Sheridan. It was armed with a 105mm gun and weighed about 25 tons. The AGS eventually emerged as the M8 Buford, only to be canceled for budgetary reasons in 1995 before serial production. (US Army)

had established conversations with Britain over the Burlington armour being developed at Chobham, and this led to improvements in the Leopard 2 armor package with a type of NERA being adopted.

In 1977, the Bundeswehr decided to begin production of the Leopard 2 tanks with the new Rheinmetall 120mm gun. More than a year was spent to settle remaining technical issues including the configuration of the fire control system. The first production batch began delivery in October 1979, sometimes called Leopard 2A0. The second production batch of the upgraded Leopard 2A1 tanks introduced a thermal imaging gunner's sight. The Leopard 2A4 introduced in December 1985 included a series of upgrades including a digital ballistic computer. There were a number of production changes during Leopard 2A4 production, but these changes did not result in a new designation. Earlier batches of tanks were later rebuilt with the digital ballistic computer and were redesignated as the Leopard 2A4 regardless of other features.

Leopard 2 series production			
Type	Batch	Production	Quantity
Leopard 2A0	1	1979–82	380
Leopard 2A1	2	1982–83	450
Leopard 2A1	3	1983–84	300
Leopard 2A2*	-	1984–87	-
Leopard 2A3	4	1984–85	300
Leopard 2A4	5	1985–87	370
Leopard 2A4	6	1988–89	150
Leopard 2A4	7	1989–90	100
Leopard 2A4	8	1991–92	75
			2,125

*Leopard 2A2 was the Leopard 2A0 rebuilt to Leopard 2A1 standards

The Leopard 2 had some success in the export market, with 445 Leopard 2s sold to the Netherlands starting in 1982. Switzerland decided to buy 380 Leopard 2A4s with the first 35 delivered in 1987 by Germany and the remainder being license built in Switzerland. Following the end of the Cold War, the Leopard 2 was widely exported within NATO owing to the German and Dutch disposal of tanks due to the reduction in the size of their armies.

A Leopard 2A4 of Panzerbataillon 33 at the Dutch Groep Geleide Wapens at De Peel Air Base in the mid-1980s. (Nederlands Institut voor Militaire Historie)

UK
Challenger 1
In the early 1970s, Britain began to examine the potential incorporation of Burlington NERA into the Chieftain as the Chieftain Mark 5/2 (FV4211), roughly in parallel with the Leopard 2 and M1 Abrams. As mentioned previously, Britain discussed a joint FMBT effort with Germany in the early 1970s but this floundered by 1977.

In December 1974, Britain received a contract from Iran for 1,200 improved Chieftain tanks. The

FV4030 Shir Iran (Lion of Iran) was based on the FV4211, and incorporated Pageant, a version of Burlington armor. The Shir had numerous improvements over Chieftain including a new powerpack, the Improved Fire Control System, hydropneumatic suspension and other features. In the event, the fall of the Shah of Iran led to a cancelation of the order in February 1979 prior to any deliveries. A significant amount of manufacture had already taken place and in late 1979, Jordan ordered 274 FV4030/2 tanks under the name Khalid MBT.

A pair of Dutch Leopard 2A4NL tanks in hull-down position behind a berm during training in the early 1990s. The Netherlands Army was the first export customer for the Leopard 2, ordering 445 tanks in 1979. These were original Leopard 2A1 tanks built in the slightly modified 2NL configuration such as the Dutch smoke dischargers. They were upgraded to the Leopard 2A4NL in 1985–87. (Nederlands Institut voor Militaire Historie)

The end of the FMBT project in 1977 led the British Army to begin the design of MBT-80 that was aimed to reach production by the late 1980s, a decade later than the M1 Abrams and Leopard 2. In September 1979, the British government decided to accelerate this process and procure a limited number of FV4030/3s. This took advantage of the development work that had already taken place for the Shir and Khalid. Named Challenger, the tank was powered by a Condor 1,200hp diesel engine and featured hydrogas suspension. The British Army considered switching to the German 120mm gun, but stuck with an Ordnance 120mm rifled gun, the L11A5; the Challenger's night fighting sensors initially relied on image intensification sights. The initial order was for 243 tanks to equip four regiments. Due to the extensive development work on Shir and Khalid, the first Challenger tanks were delivered quickly to the British Army in April 1983. The design was successful enough that the production program was extended to 426 tanks that were manufactured through 1990. The Challenger underwent continual improvements during production, including the introduction of the Barr & Stroud Thermal Observation and Gunnery System (TOGS) that entered service in 1986–87.

In the late 1980s, Britain again promoted a possible joint UK/Germany future main battle tank as the FMBT-2000 to replace the Challenger and Leopard 2. In the meantime, Vickers had acquired the Royal Ordnance factory at Leeds and promoted the idea of a Challenger 2 based on the existing Challenger chassis, but fitted with the turret and gun system of their proposed Vickers Mark 7 export tank.

E **LEOPARD 2A1, 2./PZ.BTL.244, CAT '85, BERGEN-HOHNE, FRG, 1985**
During the 1985 Canadian Army Trophy, one of the platoons of 2./Pz.Btl.244 was the high scorer of the competition and 2.Kompanie as a whole was the second-highest scoring company. This company, unlike other competitors, did not have any special competition markings aside from using a larger battalion insignia on the right rear of the turret. Otherwise, the markings followed the usual pattern with registration numbers front and rear, NATO-style tactical markings and bridging circles in grey on the front, and the national insignia on the turret side. In 1984, the Bundeswehr began switching from the previous monotone green to a new three-color camouflage scheme consisting of: RAL 6031 Bronzegrün, RAL 8027 Lederbraun, and RAL 9021 Teerschwarz. This scheme was later adopted by several other armies as part of a NATO standardization process.

2.IPz Btl 244

The prospects for a new tank were accelerated by the disappointing performance of the Challenger in the joint NATO–Canadian Army Trophy gunnery exercise in 1987. The British team came in last in CAT '87 against the M1 Abrams and Leopard 2 with the antiquated fire control system widely blamed. There was considerable political pressure both within the British government and the British Army to adopt an improved tank. Consideration was given to the M1A1 Abrams, Leopard 2, Leclerc, or the proposed Vickers Challenger 2.

In the early 1990s, the Austrian Army decided to replace its M60A1 and M60A3 tanks with 114 Leopard 2A4s from surplus Dutch stocks. Austrian crews of Panzerbataillon 14 took top honors in the Strong Europe Tank Challenge at the Grafenwöhr training area in Germany in May 2016. (US Army photo, Spc. Nathanael Mercado)

There was considerable political resistance to buying a foreign tank, and the excellent performance of the Challenger during the 1991 Gulf War helped cement the Challenger 2 as the next British tank. Furthermore, the end of the Cold War in 1990–91 significantly diminished the urgency of the program due to the downsizing of the British Army. Vickers was awarded a production contract for the Challenger 2 (FV4034) in June 1991. The first tanks were delivered in July 1994 and the last of 386 tanks in 2002.

Stillbrew Chieftain

By the mid-1970s, the Chieftain Mark 5 was the backbone of the British Army of the Rhine's tank force. An upgrade program was under way under the Totem Pole program to standardize the Mark 5/4 features on the older sub-variants. So, the Chieftain Mark 6 was the earlier Mark 2 with Totem Pole while Marks 7 and 8 were the upgraded Mark 3 tanks. Chieftain Mark 9 combined these upgrades with tank fire control modifications enabling use of new APFSDS ammunition. The Chieftain's continual upgrade program was necessary due to the discouraging demise of replacements such as FMBT and MBT-80.

Confrontations between Iraq T-62 and T-72 tanks with Iranian Chieftains during the Iran–Iraq War in the early 1980s revealed that the Chieftain was vulnerable to frontal penetration of the turret by the Soviet tank guns. There was the presumption that Soviet APFSDS ammunition would improve during the 1980s requiring at least the equivalent of 480mm of rolled homogenous armor (RHA) to prevent penetration. The proposed Chieftain Mark 5/2 was fitted with a new turret based on the new Burlington armour but this was

 CHIEFTAIN MARK 10, C SQUADRON, 14TH/20TH KING'S HUSSARS, BERLIN BRIGADE, BERLIN, 1989

The Berlin Armoured Squadron of the Berlin Brigade had adopted an "Urban Camouflage Pattern" developed by the squadron commander of 4th/7th Dragoon Guards, Maj Clendon Daukes in 1982. The camouflage colors were locally sourced in Germany and consisted of RAL 9010 white, RAL 7031 blue-grey, and RAL 8025 brown, applied in rectangular patterns. This tank, census number 00FC15, has the usual unit markings including the regimental insignia of the 14/20 H on the front of the searchlight cover, the Berlin Brigade insignia on the left front mudguard and the Union Jack on the right front mudguard. There were bright yellow/red fluorescent reflector panels applied on the hull rear as traffic warning.

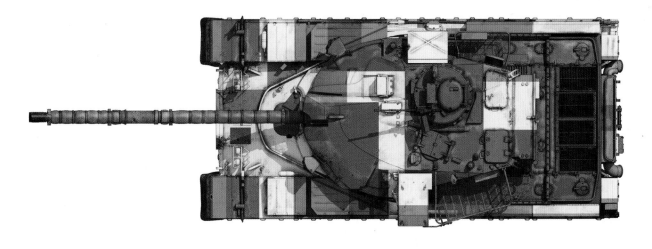

Chieftain Mark 10/C tanks of the Berlin Brigade take part in the Allied Forces Day parade on Sunday June 18, 1989 in West Berlin with the Siegessäule (Victory Column) in the background. This configuration of the Chieftain is fitted with the Stillbrew armor upgrade. (US DoD)

considerably more expensive than adding an appliqué to existing tanks. However, Burlington armour was not suitable as an appliqué to the existing Chieftain due to the complex shape of the Chieftain's cast turret. Instead, alternative configurations of an appliqué armour package using a spaced armor entered trials starting in 1982. By 1984, a suitable cast steel appliqué had been developed called the Stillbrew Crew Protection Package (SCPP), named after Colonel Still and John Brewer from the Military Vehicles and Engineering Establishment (MVEE). This consisted of a cast appliqué module averaging 300mm thick with an outer cast homogenous shell about 115mm thick, a cavity filled with six layers of rubber, and a final inner shell of cast steel armor averaging 125mm thick. The turret SCPP added 2,000kg to the tank's weight, but proved highly effective in defending the Chieftain in the frontal arc. The turret ring was protected by appliqué added on either side of the driver. The SCPP was first applied to the Chieftain Mark 9 in 1986, creating the Mark 10. The next major Chieftain upgrade was the TOGS sight, previously developed for the Challenger. The combination of TOGS and Stillbrew resulted in the definitive Chieftain Mark 11 with the upgrades applied through the early 1990s.

France
Leclerc

France began examining an Engin Principal de Combat (EPC) in 1977 to replace the AMX30B. With the collapse of the UK/Germany FMBT program in 1977, Germany raised the issue of a joint program with France developing the turret and Germany the chassis. This effort was short lived. In the meantime, the GIAT firm had developed the AMX32 for the export market that introduced a new turret using rolled armor plates rather than the cast turret of the AMX30B. In addition, the AMX32 had other upgrades, notably a new fire control system. The French Army felt that AMX32 was more expensive than an upgrade to the AMX30B while at the same time not a sufficient leap forward for the EPC requirement. GIAT continued further evolution of the design in 1983 as the AMX40 that had a new 1,100hp engine and a 120mm gun. This was aimed primarily at Saudi Arabia and Egypt, but it was also offered as an off-the-shelf solution to the French Army. In 1986, the French Army decided to move forward with a completely new design, armed with a

The Char Leclerc entered production at the very end of the Cold War in 1990–91. This Leclerc Batch 4 tank, Sgt Rivoalen (6954-0017), was upgraded later to Leclerc S1 RT4 standards.

120mm gun, and incorporating NERA protection. Unlike Germany, France decided to stay within the 50-tonne weight class. This resulted in a tank somewhat smaller than the Leopard 2. One method used to reduce volume was to use an autoloader in the turret bustle. Ammunition was limited to 40 rounds, 22 in the autoloader and the rest in the hull.

The EPC was named Leclerc after Gen Philippe Leclerc who led the French 2nd Armored Division in World War II. A testbed of the tank was completed at the AMX plant at Satory in 1986 and the first production series tanks were completed in 1991. This chronology placed the Leclerc at the outer edge of Cold War tank development.

The AMX30B and AMX30B2 remained the backbone of the French tank force through the end of the Cold War until the Leclerc finally began appearing. This is an upgraded AMX30B "Lt Desjonquères" of the 1/507 RCC in the NATO 3-color camouflage. It was originally a Batch 1 tank built in 1982, but subsequently rebuilt to the later AMX30B standards.

AMX30B

With the EBC at least a decade from production, the French Army decided to upgrade the AMX30B rather than buy an interim solution such as the AMX32 or AMX40. The AMX30B2 incorporated powerplant upgrades as well as the COTAC fire control system from the AMX32. The AMX30B2 was fitted with an image intensification camera in an armored box on the right side of the gun mantlet, replacing the active infrared searchlight previously used. The first tanks were delivered in 1981, based on AMX30B components. The AMX30B2 was ordered in three batches totaling 166 tanks and delivered in 1983–87. To reduce costs, four more batches of AMX30B2 were created by rebuilding about 600 older AMX30Bs through the early 1990s. Another life extension program began in the early 1990s, the AMX30B2 Brennus, but conversion did not begin until 1995, outside the scope of this book.

NATO MBT inventories, 1990–91										
	M47	M48	M60	M1	Leo 1	Leo 2	Centurion	Chieftain	Challenger	AMX30
Belgium					334					
Canada					114					
Denmark					330	216				
France										1,349
Germany		648			2,054	2,024				
Greece	396	1,220			109					154
Italy			300		920					
Netherlands					468	445				
Norway		55			78					
Portugal	60	86								
Spain	329	164								249
Turkey	523	3,110			150					
UK							38	850	426	
USA*		1,013	7,536	7,036						
Total	**1,308**	**6,296**	**7,836**	**7,036**	**4,557**	**2,469**	**254**	**850**	**426**	**1,752**

*About 5,160 US tanks in Europe based on CFE treaty declaration

TANKS IN BATTLE

Although there was never a direct NATO vs Warsaw Pact confrontation, there were several wars during this period that strongly affected tank technology. The 1982 war in Lebanon was the first war in which explosive reactive armor (ERA) was used in combat. As a consequence of the 1973 Middle-East War, where antitank missiles and rockets proved especially lethal, Israel had developed Blazer reactive armor. The successful use of Blazer in 1982 encouraged the adoption of ERA worldwide, most notably in the Soviet Union. The 1982 war was also the first in which both sides used tanks fitted with special armor, the Syrian T-72 and the Israeli Merkava tanks.

The other technical lesson of the 1982 war was the growing importance of armor-piercing fin-stabilized discarding-sabot (APFSDS) tank projectiles. The advent of ERA and special armors undermined the effectiveness of the high-explosive antitank (HEAT) warheads as used on antitank missiles, rocket propelled grenades, and tank gun ammunition, encouraging the use of kinetic energy projectiles such as APFSDS.

The Soviet war in Afghanistan in the 1980s provided a few technical lessons. Since the Afghan Mujahidin had no tanks, the main threat to Soviet tanks were mines and antitank rockets such as the RPG-7. The Soviet Army relied primarily on older types of tanks in Afghanistan, mainly the T-55 and T-62. These were not adequately protected against either mines or RPG-7s, leading to the adoption of appliqué armor. As mentioned earlier, NII Stali developed a kit to upgrade the older tanks that included anti-mine belly armor as well as turret and hull armor to deal with the RPG-7 threat.

The immediate response to the antitank missile threat was the application of first-generation explosive reactive armor such as Blazer and Kontakt-1. This was already in widespread service by the early 1980s since it could be added as an appliqué to existing tanks. More advanced passive "special armors" were already under development by Soviet engineers at NII Stali and British engineers at Chobham. This was used on the new generation of main battle tanks that appeared in the early 1980s.

MBT characteristics

Type	T-72A	T-64B	T-80B	M1	Leopard 2
IOC	1979	1976	1978	1980	1979
Weight (tonnes)	41.5	39.0	42.9	54.5	55.2
Crew	3	3	3	4	4
Length (m)	9.53	9.22	9.65	9.7	9.67
Width (m)	3.59	3.41	3.52	3.66	3.7
Height (m)	2.19	2.17	2.19	2.4	2.48
Engine	V-46-6	5TDF	GTD-1000T	AGT-1500	MB-875Ka501
Type	diesel	diesel	gas turbine	gas turbine	diesel
HP	780	700	1,000	1,500	1,500
HP/T	18.8	17.9	23.3	27.5	27.2
Max. speed (km/h)	60	60.5	70	72	
Gun	2A46	2A46-2	2A46-1	M68	Rh-44
Caliber (mm)	125	125	125	105	120
Ammunition	44	36	38	55	42

The largest tank battles involving NATO armies took place during the 1990–91 Gulf War that pitted a coalition led by the United States against the Iraqi Army. The tank-vs-tank fighting was extremely one-sided, in large measure due to the destruction of portions of the Iraqi forces by preliminary air attacks, the poor quality of Iraqi training and tactical leadership, and deficiencies in equipment.[1] The best Iraqi tanks were the T-72M and T-72M1, many imported from Poland. These were inferior to the premium Soviet tanks in Germany at the end of the Cold War such as the T-64B or T-80B. The T-72M1 had an early generation of special armor, but it was completely inadequate when faced by contemporary NATO APFSDS ammunition such as the US Army's M829A1 "Silver Bullet" APFSDS or the British 120mm rifled gun. In contrast, Iraqi T-72 tanks were armed with older export ammunition such as the 3BM-10 APFSDS with a short steel penetrator. This ammunition could not frontally penetrate the M1A1 Abrams at usual combat ranges.

The 1991 tank fighting also revealed the alarming tendency of the T-72 to "lose its top" when internal ammunition fires ignited the ammunition. Although usually attributed to the ammunition stored

The Italian Army developed the C1 Ariete main battle tank in the late 1980s, with deliveries beginning in the early 1990s. These two tanks belonged to the 8th Tank Battalion "M.O. Secchiaroli," 132nd Tank Regiment and are seen here at the Grafenwöhr training area in Germany during their participation in the Strong Europe Tank Challenge in May 2016. (US Army photo, Spc Nathanael Mercado)

---

1   For more detail, see: Steven Zaloga, *M1 Abrams vs T-72 Ural: Operation Desert Storm 1991* (Osprey Duel 109), 2009.

G

LEOPARD 2NL, C-ESKADRON, 43E TANKBATALJON, NORTHAG TEAM, CAT '87, BERGEN-HOHNE, FRG, 1987

The Dutch participation in the 1987 Canadian Army Trophy was from C Squadron, 43rd Tank Battalion. The Dutch participants had done well in 1985, and in 1987 one of the platoons was the top scorer from the NORTHAG (Northern Army Group) teams. The Dutch Leopards had special markings for the competition, including the national colors across the radiator vents in the rear, and a special marking adopted by the team for CAT '87 showing a Leopard. This particular tank has the name "CONQUERER" on the turret side. The other markings are the usual style including the registration plate on the rear, a yellow rectangle with the number 83-KP-07. The color scheme is overall RAL 6014 Gelboliv.

In the late 1970s, the Spanish Army began modernizing its older M48 tanks to the newer M48A5E1 and M48E2 standards including the 105mm gun and AVDS-1790-2A engines. This example is seen here during the joint Crisex '83 maneuvers with US forces. (US DoD)

in the ammunition carousel under the turret, this was only partly to blame. Only about half the ammunition was stored in the carousel and the rest in the turret and hull. What often occurred was that one of the exposed ammunition rounds was ignited when the tank armor was penetrated, which in turn led to other rounds catching fire before the conflagration finally spread to the carousel. This problem was shared by the other Soviet Triplet tanks as became so evident in the 2022 Ukraine war.

Much of the Iraqi tank force consisted of older types such as the T-55, T-62, and Chinese equivalents including the Type 59 and Type 69. The technical superiority of tanks of the Allied coalition was amplified by superior crew training and far better tactical performance.

There were a few technical curiosities unveiled during the Gulf War. A number of Iraqi T-55 and Type 69-II tanks were upgraded with a NERA appliqué, variously dubbed Enigma or Khafji armor by NATO intelligence. The Iraqi name for these improved tanks was Al-Najm (star) or Al-Faw, named after the battle of Al-Faw during the Iran–Iraq war. This armor consisted of a multi-layer sandwich of steel, aluminum, and rubber plates in a steel container, similar to some of the early forms of special armor. This upgrade was locally manufactured, but the source of this technology is not clear. It may have been provided to Iraq from the Soviet Union or China.

TECHNICAL ANALYSIS

In the wake of the 1973 Middle-East War, political pundits and journalists proclaimed that "The tank is dead." The proliferation of antitank missiles and their inexpensive cousins, the rocket-propelled grenade, suggested that the tank was no longer the dominant weapon on the modern battlefield.

This viewpoint was not shared by military professionals who realized that one wave of technological innovation usually spurred a technological counterrevolution. This was certainly the case with tank technology in the late 1970s and 1980s. This era saw a flourishing of new concepts, most notably with the advent of new types of armored protection. In addition, the new armor prompted the development of much more powerful and accurate tank guns.

The technological revolution in tank design in the 1980s resulted in a generation of main tanks that have remained the premier tanks for more than three decades. Although the T-72B, T-80U, M1A1 Abrams, Challenger, Leopard 2, and Leclerc have undergone continual upgrades since 1990, no major army has adopted a major new tank design since 1990. Several new main battle tanks have been designed since 1990, but none has been adopted in significant numbers. Tank technology reached an engineering plateau in the early 1990s when the demise of the Soviet Union deflated the Cold War arms race in Europe.

Protection

The advent of explosive reactive armor and non-energetic reactive armor complicates any short description of tank defense in this period. Tanks in the 1975–90 era went from conventional rolled and cast homogenous steel armor, to a mixture of conventional armor plus ERA or passive appliqués, and finally to a mixed configuration of conventional armor with NERA packages protecting the frontal quadrant and conventional steel armor elsewhere. The most complicated examples are the late Soviet types which had mixed configurations of NxRA, NERA, ERA and conventional armor. The tanks of the late 1980s were extremely well protected in the frontal quadrant by these new arrays as is summarized by a chart from Russian sources shown here.

The first combat use of the M60A1 with Appliqué Armor took place during Operation *Desert Storm* in 1991. The US Marine Corps deployed this kit on the M60A1 tanks of the 1st and 3rd Tank Battalions, in this case, a dozer-equipped tank.

Frontal protection of MBTs of the late 1980s (mm, RHA equivalent)		
	vs APFSDS	**vs HEAT**
T-72B		
Turret	520	950
Hull	530	900
T-80U		
Turret	780	1,320
Hull	780	1,080
M1A1		
Turret	600	700
Hull	600	700
M1A1HA		
Turret	800	1,300
Hull	600	700

Although the tanks of the late 1980s were extremely well protected in the frontal quadrants, their side, top, and rear quadrants were less well protected to avoid making the tanks impossibly heavy. As a result, tanks may have been nearly invulnerable in a frontal engagement, but the other aspects remained vulnerable to a variety of weapons. In the never-ending contest of tank vs antitank technologies, the infantry response to the new generation of tanks was a new generation of antitank missiles such as Javelin and TOW-2B. The new missiles took advantage of advanced microprocessors and sensors to aim the warhead at the vulnerable top surfaces of the tank, avoiding the best-defended areas. This innovation in turn led to the development of active protection systems (APS) for the tanks, a contest that is still under way today. Active protection systems consist of sensors to detect an inbound missile, and a munition to defeat the missile before it strikes the tank. The first of these was the Soviet Drozd system, but they did not become widespread until the 2000s, such as the Israeli Trophy system.

Firepower

The 1982 Lebanon War showed that the early APFSDS kinetic energy projectile could defeat existing homogenous armor and early generations of passive sandwich armor such as the glacis plate of the T-72. This type of ammunition underwent a rapid evolution in the 1980s, starting with short steel arrows and moving on to long-rod penetrators, often with a core of heavier and denser material such as tungsten carbide or depleted uranium. It was not until the early 1990s that APFSDS projectiles had a high probability of penetrating the hardest of the new tanks. In the 1980s, the US Army was shocked to find that even the best 105mm APFSDSs would not penetrate even export T-72 tanks. Likewise, in the early 1990s, firing tests against the T-72B's special armor found that 120mm projectiles could not penetrate the improved armors from the late 1980s. As can be seen in the accompanying chart, the power of APFSDS projectiles increased rapidly through the 1980s. (It should be noted that performance data on many of these rounds remains classified and the figures here are based on available public sources and should be treated with a bit of skepticism.)

A Challenger 1 Mark 3 named Belfast (79 KF 12) of the 14th/20th King's Hussars from the block of 60 built from May 1987 to July 1988. It is seen here in Duxford in 1990 before participating in Operation *Granby*. After the Gulf War, this particular tank served with the Queen's Royal Hussars and Queen's Dragoon Guards, eventually ending up in Jordanian service.

Estimated APFSDS performance in the 1980s (2,000m, RHA, vertical)				
Type	**Caliber (mm)**	**Army**	**IOC**	**Penetration (mm)**
3BM-15	125	USSR	1972	400
M735	105	USA	1975	250
3BM-22 Zakolka	125	USSR	1976	430
M774	105	USA	1979	380
DM23	120	Germany	1982	420
3BM-29 Nadfil-2	125	USSR	1983	430
M833	105	USA	1983	470
M827	120	USA	1984	500
3BM-32 Vant	125	USSR	1985	430
M829	120	USA	1986	560
3BM-42 Mango	125	USSR	1986	440
DM33	120	Germany	1987	480
M829A1	120	USA	1990	730
M829A2	120	USA	1992	850

The combat debut for the Challenger 1 tanks was Operation *Granby* in Iraq in 1991. This is a Challenger 1 Mark 3 of the Royal Scots Dragoon Guards, 7th Armoured Brigade.

Although APFSDS became the dominant type of ammunition for tank-vs-tank fighting, HEAT remained in widespread service. It was a more versatile type of ammunition and useful both for attacking lightly armored targets such as armored infantry vehicles as well as traditional non-armored targets such as vehicles, structures and earthworks. Tanks during this period tended to carry a mixture of APFSDS and HEAT depending on the tactical circumstances.

There were considerable advances in fire controls during the 1980s including the adoption of digital ballistic computer, thermal imaging sights, and multi-axis gun stabilization. This improved accuracy and reduced engagement time.

A comparison of the tank scores at the 1987 Canadian Army Trophy gives a sense

A remarkable photograph of an APFSDS projectile in flight as the aluminum sabot petals peel away from the long-rod penetrator. The sabot holds the small diameter penetrator centered in the gun tube during the firing process. (US Army)

of advantages of the new fire controls. The Belgian Leopard 1 tanks did better than might be expected since they had been upgraded with thermal sleeves for their guns and a new SABCA fire control system. The performance of the Challenger at CAT '87 was disappointing. While the design of the Leopard 2 and M1 Abrams fire control systems had started from scratch, the Challenger fire controls were an evolution of the older Chieftain fire controls. A British tanker who test-fired the M1A1 Abrams at CAT '89 recalled the advantages between the Abrams and Challenger: "The sighting and firing sequence and the [Abrams] gun control equipment is again really slick and simple to use. There is no complex graticule, no ellipse, no auto-lay, etc. All the gunner has to do is lay a circle on the target, press one button on the joystick gunner's control, then immediately press the adjacent firing button – shouting 'on the way' at the same time!"

Gunnery performance at CAT '87		
Type	Percentage of hits	Avg. engagement time(s)
IPM1 Abrams	94	9.1
Leopard 2	92	9.6
Leopard 1	85	11.1
Challenger	75	12.6

In general, NATO outpaced the Soviet Union in fire controls. The Soviet Union introduced laser rangefinders around the same time as NATO. However, deployment of advanced night fighting sensors was much slower, especially thermal imaging sights that were never adopted in significant numbers.

A tank thermal sight image differs from conventional optical images in that slightly warmer areas show up with greater intensity than cooler areas. So, this image of an M1 tank in motion shows the wheels and tracks as hotter due to their motion. The gun tube and engine deck are also more visible than the hull due to their greater infrared emissions. (US Army)

Combat effectiveness

In view of the large number of different tanks covered in this short book, it is hard to make detailed comparisons in such a short space. Fortunately, there was a good deal of operational research being done in the 1980s both in the Soviet Union and NATO that provides a few thumbnail assessments of the comparative effectiveness of the

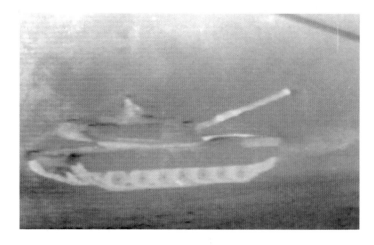

tanks of this era. These assessments attempted to create a mathematical model to determine the likely battlefield effectiveness of various types of weapons. In the case of tanks, the assessments typically revolved around firepower, mobility, protection, and command and control. Generally, a single type of tank was selected as the baseline and given a value of "1." The other tanks were then rated on a scale relative to the baseline tank.

The first two tables here are based on Soviet tank-industry data and compare NATO vs Soviet tanks from the late 1970s and mid-1980s. In both cases, the baseline tank was a version of the T-72 tank.

Combat effectiveness of late 1970s tanks *(Soviet estimates)*				
Tank	T-72A	T-80B	Leopard 2A1	M1 Abrams
IOC	1979	1978	1979	1980
	1.0	1.15	1.99	1.72

Combat effectiveness of mid-1980s tanks *(Soviet estimates)*				
Tank	T-72B	T-80U	M1A1 Abrams	Challenger
IOC	1984	1986	1985	1985
	1.0	1.15	1.54	1.31

Some broader surveys of Cold War tanks were undertaken to provide underlying data for computer-based wargame systems. The Soviet estimates were prepared by offices of the General Staff of the Soviet Army and used the T-55A as the baseline example. The US Weapon Effectiveness Indices (WEI) were prepared by the US Army's Concepts Analysis Agency, later the Center for Army Analysis. The US Army used the M60A1 as the baseline tank. It is however less detailed as many of these assessments remain classified.

A German Leopard 1A1A1 taking part in Confident Enterprise, a phase of the Reforger '83 exercise on September 28, 1983. This version was gradually upgraded in the late 1980s with thermal sights and laser rangefinders. (US DoD)

It will be noticed that the Soviet General Staff assessment judges the T-80U as significantly more effective than the M1A1 Abrams, yet the Soviet tank-industry comparison presented earlier expresses a very different opinion. These assessments are outdated and far from definitive, but at least provide an interesting starting point for evaluating the tank designs of this era.

Combat effectiveness of NATO/Warsaw Pact tanks		
	USSR	USA
Centurion (105mm)	0.79	1.0
T-55A	1.0	0.75
Leopard 1A1	1.06	n/a
T-62	1.07	0.9
M48A5	1.12	0.9
AMX30B2	1.13	1.1
Chieftain Mark 5	1.15	1.05
T-55M	1.17	n/a
M60A1	1.25	1.0
M60A2	1.25	n/a
M60A3	1.26	1.15
Leopard 1A4	1.29	1.05
T-64A	1.5	1.25
T-72A	1.55	1.2
M1	1.73	1.5
Challenger	1.88	1.45
T-64B	2.0	n/a
M1A1	2.0	1.55
Leopard 2	2.03	1.5
T-72B1	2.06	n/a
T-80B	2.17	1.45
T-80U	2.57	n/a

FURTHER READING

There are numerous monographs dealing with specific tank types of this era such as the Osprey New Vanguard series. This reading list avoids these due to their sheer number and instead highlights broader national surveys.

Beckmann, Heinrich, *Schild und Schwert: Die Panzertruppe der Bundeswehr-Geschichte einer Truppengattung*, Podzun-Pallas, Friedberg: 1989.

Cameron, Robert, *The Canadian Army Trophy: Achieving Excellence in Tank Gunnery*, Armor School, Fort Benning: 2018.

Feskov, V.I., et al., *Sovetskaya armiya v gody "kholodnoy voyny" 1945–1991*, Tomskiy Gos. Universitet, Tomsk: 2004.

Francev, Vladimír, *Československé tankové síly 1945–1992*, Grada, Prague: 2012.

Magnuski, Janusz, *Wozy bojowe LWP 1943–1983*, WMON, Warsaw: 1985.

Spielberger, Walter, et al., *Die Kampfpanzer der NVA*, Motorbuch, Stuttgart: 1996.

Ustyantsev, Sergei, and Kolmakov, D., *T-72/T-90: Opyt sozdaniya otechestvennikh osnovnikh boevykh tankov*, Media-Print, Nizhni-Tagil: 2013.

Zolotarev, V.A. (ed.), *Rossiya (SSSR) v lokalnykh voynakh i voennykh konfliktakh vtoroy poloviny XX veka*, Kulikovo Pole, Moscow: 2000.

INDEX

Note: Page locators in **bold** refer to plate captions, pictures and illustrations.